# FOREWORD

BY

JOSH MCDOWELL

*FIRST, CONGRATULATIONS FOR PICKING UP* this book. While most people are curious about Jesus, they aren't eager to be seen carrying around a book with his name on the cover. Plus, the idea of taking a dare is also a bit uncomfortable. Isn't taking a dare something kids did back in middle school?

Second, I'd like to say I can relate to your quest. Every individual needs to decide what to do with the claims of Jesus. I took my own Jesus dare years ago at university. I remember it like it was yesterday.

In my search for freedom and purpose, I had tried just about everything—from sampling religion to building my own reputation. Religion left me empty. Maybe I chose the wrong church. Partying on weekends left me in pain. Maybe I chose the wrong crowd. On campus I had earned some power and prestige, but nothing filled the hole in my heart.

Then I noticed a small group of students and professors who seemed to know why they believed what they believed. That was appealing to me. I started asking questions. Lots of them. The answers I found led to a life-changing decision and an international ministry I could have never imagined.

The undeniable truths I uncovered and my personal journey to trusting Christ as Savior and Lord are told in *More Than a Carpenter*. That little book—about the size of this book—has been translated into more than 100 languages with more than 30 million copies in print. It has been distributed in more than 150 countries, many where it's illegal to own a copy.

The author of this book, Jay Payleitner, was with me in Moscow shortly before the dissolution of the Soviet Union. As the radio producer for "Josh McDowell Radio," Jay was part of the team handing out copies of the Russian translation of *More Than a Carpenter* in and around Red Square. Jay tells me that experience in 1991 was a catalyst to his writing career which has led directly to *The Jesus Dare*.

Decades ago I wrote *More Than a Carpenter* on twelve legal pads in 48 hours. My goal was to write

down everything I would say to a seeking friend over a cup of coffee if he asked, "Why should I believe in Jesus?"

Jay wrote *The Jesus Dare* over the course of a year on his MacBook Pro. But the questions remain the same: *Who is Jesus?* and *How should I respond?*

DEDICATED TO:
ALL SEEKERS, REBELS,
FREE THINKERS, QUESTIONERS,
AND PRODIGALS. THE ONES
I KNOW. AND THOSE I MAY
NOT MEET FOR A WHILE.

—JAY PAYLEITNER

# WELCOME

### HEY THERE, READY FOR AN ADVENTURE?

Of course, I'm not sure what brought you here, what your goal might be.

It could simply be a healthy curiosity on your part. You've set out to consider the many theories of why humans exist and how to make the most of our lives, and Christianity is on that list. That's a noble quest.

It could be that you're reading this book only because it was a gift from a thoughtful, caring friend who wanted to provide you with a nonthreatening way to consider the claims of Christ. You may or may not be expecting much. But I promise the hour or two you invest will be worth your while. That's a noble quest, and worthy of your best efforts.

This book could be an unexpected gift directly from the Creator of the universe. You just happened to run across it on Amazon or an airport bookrack, and God nudged you. That's a good sign. It means He's after you.

In any case, I hope you keep an open mind and open heart to this singular idea: *Jesus' story is your story.* You are why God sent His Son to earth. This book unpacks that idea in a way you probably have never heard before. Okay?

Those who trust in
the Lord will find
new strength. They
will soar high on
wings like eagles.
They will run and not
grow weary. They will
walk and not faint.

—ISAIAH 40:31 NLT

"For I know the plans I have for you," declares the Lord, "plans to prosper you and not to harm you, plans to give you hope and a future."

*—JEREMIAH 29:11*

EVERY ADVENTURE BEGINS
WITH A CURIOUS MIND
AND BECKONING HEART.

—*JAY PAYLEITNER*

# THE JESUS DARE

### THE ADVENTURE
### YOU'VE BEEN WAITING FOR

## JAY PAYLEITNER

LIVE YOUR FAITH

Leave it to one of my favorite thinkers to issue the ultimate challenge for our day. Jay's dare is no trivial diversion. Enter into this only if you mean business—you might never be the same.

**JERRY JENKINS**, AUTHOR OF MORE THAN 170 PUBLISHED WORKS INCLUDING THE MEGASELLING *LEFT BEHIND* SERIES

Many think Jesus came to make us nicer people. Jay Payleitner reveals the awful, wonderful truth. God wants to do something infinitely deeper than make you nice. Take the challenge.

**CHRIS FABRY**, AUTHOR AND HOST OF CHRIS FABRY LIVE

Jay Payleitner has written many wonderful books, but this book has to be his best work to date. *The Jesus Dare* will truly bless and challenge you as you dare to grow deeper with Jesus, the One whose name is above every name. I took the challenge and was blessed. I dare you to."

**CAREY CASEY**, CEO/PRESIDENT, CHAMPIONSHIP FATHERING

This book cleverly addresses issues that have held curious minds away from Jesus, and dares them to draw near. While so many books are righteously religious, Jay's writing style is more like a conversation over the backyard fence with a curious neighbor who feels safe enough to ask questions. The reader is affirmed, informed, invited, and praised. It is a setting for success that I believe will transform hearts. Maybe even yours.

**REV. DR. JOHN P. NELSON**, SENIOR PASTOR, HOSANNA! CHURCH

Like so many people, I was skeptical and needed credible answers about life, purpose, and God. Finally, my journey led me to take a dare similar to the one described in this book and Jesus changed my life forever. *The Jesus Dare* just might bring clarity to your journey, too.

**DAVID HORSAGER**, BESTSELLING AUTHOR AND CEO, TRUST EDGE LEADERSHIP INSTITUTE

An important book to read as we face the increasing challenges of fast-paced cultural changes. *The Jesus Dare* will focus your beliefs and further equip you to bring Christ to a hurting world.

**CLAIR HOOVER**, EXECUTIVE DIRECTOR, NATIONAL COALITION OF MINISTRIES TO MEN

Sound logic. Solid truth. Simple presentation. Reading *The Jesus Dare* isn't like slugging through some deep theological thesis. Conversational and fun, *The Jesus Dare* is an all-you-can-eat buffet of how to have a life-changing relationship with Jesus—served up in delicious bite-sized chunks.

**TIM SHOEMAKER**, AUTHOR OF *THE VERY BEST, HANDS-ON, KINDA DANGEROUS FAMILY DEVOTIONS*

I love Jay's heart and boldness in issuing a challenge in a generation poised for some of the greatest kingdom exploits in history. Take the dare and join the adventure!

**MARK HANCOCK**, CEO, TRAIL LIFE USA AND AUTHOR OF *WHY ARE WE SITTING HERE UNTIL WE DIE?*

**TO**

_____

**FROM**

_____

*The Jesus Dare: The Adventure You've Been Waiting For*
Copyright © 2019 by Jay Payleitner
First Edition, May 2019

Published by:

P.O. Box 1010
Siloam Springs, AR 72761
dayspring.com

Scripture quotations marked NIV are taken from THE HOLY BIBLE, NEW INTERNATIONAL VERSION®, NIV® Copyright © 1973, 1978, 1984, 2011 by Biblica, Inc.® Used by permission. All rights reserved worldwide.

Scripture quotations marked NLT are taken from the Holy Bible, New Living Translation, copyright © 1996, 2004, 2007, 2013, 2015 by Tyndale House Foundation. Used by permission of Tyndale House Publishers, Inc., Carol Stream, Illinois 60188. All rights reserved.

Scripture quotations marked ESV are taken from The ESV® Bible (The Holy Bible, English Standard Version®). ESV® Text Edition: 2016. Copyright © 2001 by Crossway, a publishing ministry of Good News Publishers. The ESV® text has been reproduced in cooperation with and by permission of Good News Publishers. Unauthorized reproduction of this publication is prohibited. All rights reserved.

Scripture quotations marked NASB are taken from the NEW AMERICAN STANDARD BIBLE ®, © Copyright 1960, 1962, 1963, 1968, 1971, 1972, 1973, 1975, 1977, 1995 by the Lockman Foundation. Used by permission. (www.lockman.org)

Written by: Jay Payleitner
Designed and Typeset by: Greg Jackson of thinkpen.design
Printed in China
Prime: 91626
ISBN: 978-1-68408-678-8

God has prepared you to read this book. In a similar way, He prepared me to pick up a book on a Sunday evening in February of 1977 and it was then and there that I said yes to 'The Jesus Dare'. You have already picked up the book, now go ahead and do the next thing and give it a read. God be with you!

**BRIAN DOYLE**, FOUNDER AND PRESIDENT, IRON SHARPENS IRON

Jay has invested in many lives by giving us practical ways to grow closer to our children and family. Now he takes an even bigger step of helping us develop a more intimate relationship with Jesus. Take the dare! See what Christ has for you!

**DAN SEABORN**, PRESIDENT AND FOUNDER, WINNING AT HOME, INC.

Jay has a winsome way of thoughtfully pulling back the curtain of Christianity to explain the simple fundamentals of what it really means to believe in Jesus. It's a perfect tool to give a friend wrestling with the vagaries of trusting Christ. Just as Mere Christianity became a go-to primer for a "pre-Christian," I believe so will *The Jesus Dare!*

**JIM SANDERS**, EXECUTIVE VICE PRESIDENT, AMBASSADOR ADVERTISING

Wow! If you're a Christian, *The Jesus Dare* is a wonderful book, not only because it is clear, Biblical and profound...but because it does "double duty." It will remind you of the reliability of the truth you love. But then, it is a book you'll give to everybody you care about who hasn't taken the "Jesus dare." So many of them will be drawn to the throne of grace. They and you will rise up and call Jay Payleitner blessed.

**STEVE BROWN**, SEMINARY PROFESSOR, HOST OF "KEY LIFE RADIO," AND BEST-SELLING AUTHOR OF *TALKING THE WALK: HOW TO BE RIGHT WITHOUT BEING INSUFFERABLE*

Think of this book as a fitness regimen for the soul, and Jay Payleitner as your personal trainer. Read one brief chapter a day to build spiritual muscle.

**DAVID MURROW**, AUTHOR OF *WHY MEN HATE GOING TO CHURCH*

A practical guide for anyone asking the hard questions about Jesus. Give it to everyone who is truly seeking.

**GRADY HAUSER**, CONFERENCE SPEAKER AND AUTHOR OF *PASSING THE BATON*

In 1 John 2:27, John the Evangelist issued a challenge to the Early Church, "focus on following Jesus." In *The Jesus Dare*, Jay Payleitner, issues the same ancient challenge in a modern context, "don't get caught up in religion, stay focused on relationships just like Jesus." In a time when division and fraud are prevalent, this book is a path for building unifying, authentic friendships around the life and love of Jesus as we "remain in Him."

**JIM LISKE**, LEAD PASTOR, CHRIST MEMORIAL CHURCH, HOLLAND, MICHIGAN
FORMER PRESIDENT AND CEO, PRISON FELLOWSHIP MINISTRIES

# INTRODUCTION

**THE NAME OF JESUS HAS A HISTORY** of stirring up trouble. It was true when He walked this planet, and it's true today.

The words He spoke brought people together. But just as often, His words were disruptive and divisive.

It's understandable that many people don't want to put in the effort to think about Someone who lived two millennia ago. In our fast-paced world every minute matters, and we can easily be dazzled by the latest technology. Plus, it's natural for people to think, *What's in it for me?*

Looking around, you might say that Jesus isn't in fashion these days. Sure, quite a few people go to church. Christmas and Easter are still on the calendar. But you have to admit the distractions and naysayers are beginning to add up.

While His message is meant for the entire world, Jesus always knew there would be long seasons when His voice would be ignored or dismissed.

I fear we're entering one of those seasons right now. Jesus' message of love, justice, repentance, and reconciliation is being received—not with life-giving joy—but rather with indifference. Or even scorn. In some circles, identifying yourself as a Christian might lead to being mocked or belittled for being out of touch.

It won't always be that way, but that's the current status quo.

This book dares to stand up to today's dismissive, pessimistic, and narcissistic culture. We're delivering good news about values and morality that get a lot of lip service but rarely get put into practice. When that happens we miss out on virtues like peace, love, joy, kindness, respect, and self-control.

If you read carefully, these pages just might reveal your own personal roadmap for a journey of discovery and adventure.

You can also expect some edgier messages dealing with truth, justice, suffering, eternity, and the creation of the universe.

The world is in desperate need of some honest answers and divine guidance. Don't you think?

# CONTENTS

# WHAT IF HE IS WHO HE SAYS HE IS?

MATTHEW 16:15 NIV

**OUR OBJECTIVE IS CLARITY, NOT CONFUSION.** Hope, not despair. Illumination, not darkness.

The questions we're asking may be ones you have already pondered.

Who is Jesus? What makes Him different? Do Christians today really have a corner on truth? What and where is this place called heaven of which Jesus spoke? Why do some of the smartest people on the planet reject the message? What happens if I set this question aside for now and get back to it later?

To be sure, uncertainty, curiosity, and anxiety are reasonable reactions to the question of how to respond to Jesus. It's a life-or-death question that shouldn't be taken lightly. The only unacceptable reaction is indifference.

You can't ignore Jesus. He said He was the Son of God. He said the only way to heaven was through Himself. He said He would rise from the dead, ascend to be with God in heaven, and eventually come back to judge all of humankind.

You either believe Him. Or you don't.

If you reject this man called Jesus, then so be it. Unless you change your mind, your fate has been determined. If you believe in the Son of God, freely receive His message, and surrender to His will, then your fate also has been determined.

This book is for those who are on the fence or have never really considered all the evidence. These pages will help you address the one big question about Jesus that must be answered: *What if He is who He says He is?*

Ignoring this question will leave you on the outside looking in and wondering what happened. That's not a place you want to be.

All of which leads us to the dare. You can certainly stop reading anytime. But if you keep at it, you will eventually come to an ultimatum you will ultimately give to yourself. Along the way, I encourage you to consider all the facts. Ask your toughest questions. Use your brain, your heart, and that still small voice that helps you discern right from wrong. Don't let another individual or group make the decision for you. Your choice is too important.

This small book comes with a big challenge. Are you up for it? When you reach the last chapter, might you be ready to take the Jesus dare?

# MAKING
# THIS
# PERSONAL

> *Draw near to God and He will draw near to you.*

JAMES 4:8 NASB

**AS INDICATED BY THE TITLE,** this book is about Jesus. But the main character is you.

Jesus is the same yesterday, today, and tomorrow. During the writing, editing, printing, distribution, and reading of this book, Jesus will not be undergoing any life-changing insights or redefining His priorities. But you might.

After all—like everyone else on the planet—you are working your way through life and have experienced a few bumps and bruises, and maybe even some broken bones or a broken heart. For sure, you've got all kinds of gifts and abilities. You're doing pretty much okay. But something has led you to this page in this book at this time.

Since everyone is different, I can only guess at your burdens, heartaches, and fears. The possibilities are plentiful. Loss. Grief. Emptiness. Loneliness. Anger.

Distrust. Financial worries. Betrayal. Guilt. Stress. Indecision. Regret.

Or maybe you just have a restlessness or a sense there must be more to life.

As you know, the world offers a wide range of temporary hit-or-miss answers to the challenges we face. Maybe you've tried some of them: a walk in the park, a new job, a new set of friends, a gym membership, a two-year sabbatical, adopting a dozen cats, binge watching a popular TV drama, pills, pot, a torrid affair, a spending spree, a crime spree, venting on social media, moving across the country, or anything else that might numb the symptoms.

But you want to do more than just treat symptoms. You want a cure. You're not exactly sure if anything is broken, but you're still looking for a tried-and-true fix. After experimenting with several remedies that didn't work, you are ready for a more permanent solution.

Well, the answer is not as far away as you may think. Best of all, it's not based on a fleeting fad or a feel-good moment that lasts two minutes or less.

As one of God's favorites, you deserve more than that. You deserve a solution that works now and forever.

The path you're about to take will have a few curves, hills, brambles, detours, and roadblocks. But it's worth the trip. At the end of the trail, I promise your feet will find solid ground.

# JESUS' GREATEST HITS

> *Seek first His kingdom and His righteousness, and all these things will be given to you as well.*

MATTHEW 6:33 NIV

**LET'S BEGIN WITH SOME GOOD NEWS.** Some really good news.

Below is a list of verifiable benefits—long and short term—of inviting Jesus into your life. I believe it's a sensible way to launch a book that is going to ask you to take that step of faith.

1. Feeling loved like never before

2. The ability to love like never before

3. A fresh start and clean slate from all your misdeeds, regrets, and failures

4. An anchor in the storm, a rock on which to stand, a hand that calms the seas

5. An awareness and trust that even if bad stuff

happens to you—stuff you don't want to even imagine—it can all be used for good

6. In addition to a new ability to give and receive love, an endless supply of joy, peace, patience, kindness, goodness, faithfulness, gentleness, and self-control

7. 2.3 billion people you can call brother or sister

8. A hunger to know more about Jesus and the Bible

9. Insight that leads to a stronger marriage and family relationships (all relationships, really)

10. Indwelling by the Holy Spirit (a trustworthy Guide who's infinitely more reliable than your periodically impulsive conscience)

11. A surprising sense of purpose, a calling, an assignment worth your time and effort

12. Eternal life

I can already hear the pushback. *Really? That all sounds too good to be true.* Well, yeah. That's kind of the point.

We are not worthy. With our thoughts and actions, we humans push God aside and miss out on most of His good gifts. But God loves us despite that fact and sent Jesus to get us back on track.

Maybe think of it this way: You have a standing invitation to join God's family. You are on the threshold of ultimate personal fulfillment. Your salvation is a miracle on hold.

God is just waiting for each of us to say, "Count me in."

# SO, WHAT'S THE JESUS DARE?

> *For God so loved the world that He gave His one and only Son, that whoever believes in Him shall not perish but have eternal life.*

JOHN 3:16 NIV

**THE JESUS DARE IS NOT A NEW CONCEPT.** In and around Christian circles, it goes by a bunch of other names. It's a life-changing decision with eternal consequences. And it involves an investment of both your intellect and character. Your head and your heart.

It's all about having the knowledge of who Jesus is and what He accomplished through His death and resurrection. Then, secure in that knowledge, there needs to be an understanding of your own brokenness and a desire to be rescued from your imperfect condition. It's not something you can do on your own. Even your best efforts can't earn a passing grade.

Finally, in a single moment, you may find yourself choosing to put your faith in what Jesus has done on your behalf.

The moment you take the Jesus dare you will be "born again" or "saved." Said in other ways, you will have "received Christ," "come to Christ," "invited Christ into your life," or "met Christ."

A scholarly theologian might say you will have experienced "justification by the propitiatory blood of Christ."

On any Sunday, there are plenty of preachers who use the phrase "repent and believe" while they bang their fists on a pulpit to emphasize the point. I don't necessarily endorse abusing furniture, but that wording works too.

Because it helps children imagine the transaction going on, some people use the phrase "ask Jesus into your heart." I think that's a nice way of putting it, although that doesn't sit well with some pastors.

Over the years, denominations and organizations have put together specific formulas or prescripts. And they work. The "sinner's prayer" and the "four spiritual laws" have helped millions "respond to the gospel."

Some theologians insist the essential step of faith occurs anytime someone believes in the truth of

John 3:16. (See above.) That's why you will see an occasional religious zealot hoisting a banner featuring a bold and audacious "John 3:16" at rallies, races, and football games. Bedsheets with Scripture references are not my preferred method of evangelism, but I sincerely believe God can use that kind of outreach to make people curious. Whatever works, right? As long as you're not blocking anyone's view of the field.

Other popular ways to describe the Jesus dare are "putting Jesus on the throne of your life" and "receiving the gift of eternal life."

Again, these all pretty much mean the same thing. If you happen to be a Bible scholar and want to debate or disallow any specific terminology, feel free to track me down and make your case. But clearly the purpose of this book is to draw people toward a relationship with God, not erect barriers or argue biblical hermeneutics, ecclesiology, or eschatology. (Don't bother looking up those big words. The point is, we're *not* going there.)

Even the idea of "taking the Jesus dare" may be a stretch for some narrow-minded pastor sitting in a dark office filled with books that are too difficult for most of us to understand. I honor that pastor's faithful adherence to traditional biblical interpretation, but we're going to stay the course and stick with that term. After all, the phrase "Jesus dare" has gotten you to pick up this book and read this far.

# WHO
# ARE YOU
# CALLING A
# SINNER?

> All have sinned and fall short
> of the glory of God.

ROMANS 3:23 NIV

*YOU MAY HAVE NOTICED* that before you take the Jesus dare, you have to be able to identify sin, admit there is sin in your life, and renounce it.

That's easier said than done. Especially in today's culture in which anything goes and no one wants to take responsibility for anything. (That's a bit of an overstatement, but you catch my drift.)

A definition of sin might be in order. Try these on and see if they fit:

- Sin is choosing your way rather than God's way.

- Sin is any thought, statement, action, or inaction that contradicts the character of God.

- Sin is anything we do—or don't do—that breaks God's heart.

You may have noticed that you really can't define sin without bringing God into the equation. Which, of course, makes the definition *meaningless* to those who don't believe in God. Are you tracking with me? I hope so.

In a world without God—which would also be a world without eternity or moral standards—it's *impossible* to sin. How could you? There would be no standards of right or wrong. Anyone could do anything at any time.

Sure, in a world without God, you might care for and protect your family. But it wouldn't be required. You might be kind to animals. But that's your choice. You might think it's improper to kill six million Jews or fly planes into skyscrapers. But others might think that's perfectly okay. You might think child pornography is reprehensible. But the guy down the street might disagree.

You see, without God—without a dependable standard—there is no truth that applies at all times to all people. That's why it takes an understanding of who God is in order to define sin.

A brief and incomplete list describing God's character might help you know Him better. God is love, truth, mercy, respect, justice, righteousness, and peace.

So anything that is not loving or truthful is a sin. When you act without mercy or respect, that's a sin. Being unjust or dishonorable is sinful. Can you see how attitudes and actions that contradict the attributes of God help us identify sin?

A few more thoughts, then we'll move on. The immediate consequences of some sins are more severe than others, but all sins—even a fleeting thought of envy over a friend's new smartphone—contradict God's best for our lives and separate us from Him. As we get closer to God, we become more aware of our sinful condition. It's actually healthy to feel guilty for our sins.

We tend not to dwell on this idea, but it's sin—yours and mine—that led to Jesus' torturous death on a wooden cross. The Son of God, who led a perfect and blameless life, accepted His assignment to sacrifice Himself and endure the whipping, the piercing nails, the crown of thorns, and death on our behalf.

Acknowledging that sacrifice and addressing the repercussions of sin so you can live free from its bondage is the whole purpose of the Jesus dare. Hope this makes sense. It's pretty important.

# WHAT
# WAS THAT
# BIG WORD
# AGAIN?

> [Jesus] was delivered over to death
> for our sins and was raised
> to life for our justification.

ROMANS 4:25 NIV

**IN OUR ATTEMPT TO DEFINE** the Jesus dare, we tossed out a nice long word that would have been easy to blow right past: *justification.*

That word refers to what happens the moment a man or woman is acquitted—found not guilty—in the eyes of God even though he or she has sinned, is sinning, and will continue to sin.

How does justification work? I'm glad you asked.

Let me put it in the context of a series of core truths that every authentic follower of Christ has come to understand. Here are the basics in brief:

• All people sin.

• Sin separates us from God and prevents us from fully experiencing God's love.

- Someone has to pay the penalty for our sins. (Believe me, you don't want it to be you.)

- God sent His Son to earth as a gift to show us how to live and, ultimately, to pay the penalty for our sins with His death on the cross.

- Each person has the free choice to understand and accept that gift. Which, by the way, is called grace.

- Grace can't be earned. Again, it's a free gift. Once you understand and receive it, you will have been justified. (And being justified is being treated by God *just as if* you've never sinned.)

- At that moment of repentance, you can count on receiving those dozen attributes described a few pages back under "Jesus' Greatest Hits."

That's the gospel in layman's terms. You may or may not have heard it before. Feel free to bookmark this page and refer back to these seven principles.

For now, let's set them aside and keep turning pages. Because, frankly, you're not ready to make this kind of life-changing decision. (Well, you could be. As a matter of fact, that would be fantastic because then you could start reaping the benefits of having Christ in your life right away.)

But let's assume you've got a few more questions that need answering and a few more reasonable doubts to untangle. That's not a bad thing. Especially since it gives you an excuse to read the rest of this book, which describes all kinds of logical, practical, miraculous, mysterious, and obvious reasons for you to take the Jesus dare and experience justification.

Just promise not to get squashed by a giant boulder between now and then. Because where you spend eternity depends on whether or not you make a decision for Christ while you're still in this world.

# TWO
# MORE
# BIG
# WORDS

> *God has not called us for the purpose of impurity, but in sanctification.*

I THESSALONIANS 4:7 NASB

*HERE'S ANOTHER THOUGHT* you'll want to hang onto: there are three major events in the life of an authentic Christian.

1. Justification
2. Sanctification
3. Glorification

The first and last events each occur in an instant, and they bookend the middle event, which lasts much longer than just a single moment.

Justification is what happens when you accept Christ as your Savior and put Him on the throne of your life. Sanctification is a process that will take the rest of your life, and that's learning to recognize sin and trust the leading of the Holy Spirit. Glorification is meeting

God face-to-face, when His complete glory will be revealed to you.

You can see how these three experiences create a framework for the future of anyone about to take the Jesus dare. And you can also see how they correlate to the three members of the Trinity: Jesus, the Holy Spirit, and God the Father.

Didn't sign up for a theology lesson? Not to worry. Future chapters will include some additional abstract thinking, challenging statements, and soul searching. But you will come across no more five-syllable words.

(By the way, because sanctification is an ongoing *process*, you will inevitably meet Christians who say stupid things, sometimes act like jerks, and don't have all the answers. Between our justification and glorification, we're all under construction.)

# SIDENOTE
# ABOUT
# ALL THESE
# SCRIPTURE
# VERSES

**FOR THE MOMENT,** if you don't believe in the Bible, you may be getting a bit irritated. Sorry.

I've sprinkled in relevant portions of Scripture along the way for three reasons. First, the Bible is at the core of the Christian faith. Jesus is even called "the Word made flesh." Before you consider the Jesus dare, you need to know what you're getting into.

Second, I believe in the accuracy and value of the Bible. Yes, it can be confusing at times, and it can seem contradictory, outdated, outlandish, filled with unnecessary violence, or even like a fairy tale. But the more you dig through it, the clearer and more relevant it becomes.

Third, in writing this book I felt a personal responsibility to make sure each chapter was rooted in the truth of God's Word. Otherwise, what I say is meaningless.

Funny. I sincerely believe that if you finish this book and take the Jesus dare, you will be quickly drawn to flip back and reread those chapters that stirred your soul. Those short portions of Scripture—the ones you initially overlooked—will very likely become precious guideposts for your new life in Christ.

# BEING
# MADE
# NEW

> *If anyone is in Christ, he is a new creation. The old has passed away; behold, the new has come.*

*II CORINTHIANS 5:17 ESV*

**PLEASE DON'T TAKE THE JESUS DARE** hoping it'll fix one or two of your minor imperfections. Jesus is not in the business of temporary patching and mending.

He is all about transformation.

That decision we're talking about will change everything about you except your physical self. Your mind will begin to see the world differently—through the eyes of Christ. When temptation heads your direction, you'll have a new ability to distinguish right from wrong. Not only will you have an increased awareness of the needs of others, your heart will be opened to actually doing something to meet those needs! Don't be surprised if you are more patient, forgiving, joyful, and generous. That's the Holy Spirit working in you and through you.

Immediately after taking the Jesus dare, you may not *feel* any different. That's normal. There may even be a momentary sense of anxiety or pang of regret. That's Satan digging in his scaly heels because he just lost another one. (Yay for our side!)

When you look in the mirror, you also probably won't see a difference. (Although you might! There very well could be a fresh countenance staring back at you with a bit of a smile and a twinkle in the eye.)

Regrettably, quite a few things you would like to change won't be different. That includes the negative repercussions left over from your old life. Any criminal record will still be on the books. Any addiction or disease related to poor choices will still be impacting your physical self. Some of the habits you wish you could shake may still be hanging on. Relationships damaged by words or actions will still need repair.

Along with that bad news comes even worse news. Even after you have claimed victory in a new relationship with Jesus Christ, Satan is still after you. This world is still broken. Which means you will be tempted, tested, and victimized. After all, you're not yet nestled safely in your heavenly home.

In summary, Satan has gained authority over the minds of men and the ways of the world. In a one-on-one battle with that fallen angel and master deceiver, you would lose every time. But as a new creation, you will no longer be a slave to sin. The battle continues. But because of Jesus, your victory is assured.

# YOUR
# NEW
# ARSENAL

> *May the God of peace...equip you with everything good for doing His will, and may He work in us what is pleasing to Him.*

*HEBREWS 13:20–21 NIV*

**THE WAR IMAGERY MENTIONED** at the close of the previous chapter may seem a little over the top. But make no mistake, there is a battle raging for the hearts and minds of every person on the planet. In a New Testament letter written to a young man named Timothy, the apostle Paul describes the Christian life as fighting the good fight (I Timothy 6:12).

Be assured, any new warrior taking the Jesus dare will be equipped with all necessary weapons, tactics, and supplies to ultimately emerge victorious. You can expect to lose some skirmishes along the way, but the winning team has already been determined.

The most critical weapons in your arsenal include the following:

- A direct line of communication with the Creator of the universe, the Eternal King. Some call it prayer.

  *If you believe, you will receive whatever you ask for in prayer (Matthew 21:22 NIV).*


- A diverse team of fellow warriors with skills and gifts that integrate and complement your own abilities. Some call it the church. (Which, by the way, refers to people, not a building.)

  *Let us think of ways to motivate one another to acts of love and good works. And let us not neglect our meeting together, as some people do, but encourage one another, especially now that the day of His return is drawing near (Hebrews 10:24–25 NLT).*


- An even tighter group of experienced champions that have your best interest in mind. Call them mentors and elders.

  *Plans fail for lack of counsel, but with many advisers they succeed (Proverbs 15:22 NIV).*

- The desire to set aside time specifically to recognize your Designer and align your priorities with His, especially unified alongside fellow warriors. That's the purpose of worship.

> *The time is coming—indeed it's here now—when true worshipers will worship the Father in spirit and in truth. The Father is looking for those who will worship Him that way (John 4:23 NLT).*

- The Bible (God's Word, the law of the Lord, the Holy Scriptures, the Sword of the Spirit)

> *The word of God is alive and active. Sharper than any double-edged sword, it penetrates even to dividing soul and spirit, joints and marrow; it judges the thoughts and attitudes of the heart (Hebrews 4:12 NIV).*

Prayer. Fellowship. Wise counsel. Worship. The Bible itself. These are all actual tools available to you right now, even *before* you take the Jesus dare. As you move forward in your pursuit of truth, your mastery of these weapons will sharpen. Relationships—with the people in your life and your Father in heaven—will deepen. You'll gain a clearer understanding of the meaning, relevance, and nuances of hymns, passages of Scripture, sermons, and even books like this.

Your increasing proficiency with your new arsenal confirms that God wants you to step out of the shadows and enjoy an empowering sense of purpose and impact. The impact you will make during your life ultimately depends on the tools you choose to use and how you use them.

# STAND FOR
# SOMETHING

*NOT SURE WHO SAID IT,* but it's clever and accurate: "If you don't stand for something, you'll fall for anything."

Having a cause—a reason to get out of bed in the morning—is not the main benefit of taking the Jesus dare. But it's a compelling advantage and identifying trait of those who know Christ and pursue His will for their lives.

Too many people wander through life temporarily surrendering their hearts, minds, and souls to the latest trendy trend. It could be a fad religion, the social cause du jour, or whatever the brashest voice happens to endorse that month. Cleansing diets, fitness crazes, and vitamin regimens come and go. Most of these pursuits fall under the major heading of the human desire for sex and beauty, money and power, health and extended life, and—the biggest of all—freedom from any authority other than ourselves.

Persuaded by today's news headlines, spurious social media posts, and ranting radio hosts, huge numbers of humans looking for purpose converge for all kinds of marches, memorials, and movements. Some are actually worthwhile. Most are not.

Whether they are marching down Main Street or hiding in their darkened living rooms, it's abundantly clear that just about everybody is in desperate need of answers, of something or someone they can count on. After hearing all the podcasts, watching all the talking heads on television, and scanning all the news magazines, most of us are left with more and more unsettling and disturbing questions.

I'm delighted to report that authentic followers of Christ have answers. They have something unchangeable and eternal to believe in. Jesus is a rock, an unwavering firm foundation. The Bible has stood the test of time. Denominations may disagree on minor points, but the main facts don't change. Allow me to paraphrase those principles, which were spelled out in the

Nicene Creed, a profession of faith dating back to the fourth century.

There's only one God. He made everything. As prophesied in the Old Testament, God sent His only Son—fully human and fully God—to suffer, die on a cross, and be buried for our salvation. But Jesus rose from the dead, ascended into heaven, and will return in glory in the final days to take all believers to heaven. We believe in the presence of the Holy Spirit within us, we value baptism and the church, and we look forward to eternal life in heaven. Amen.

These are facts worth fighting and dying for. They are the framework for an authentic Christian faith. Even as these facts provide answers, they also invite a range of reasonable follow-up questions. But give these facts a chance and you'll find all kinds of corroborating evidence. And virtually zero evidence that invalidates these concepts.

Furthermore, adding to your knowledge base regarding these ancient truths can be wonderfully soul satisfying. Believe it or not, after taking the Jesus dare you will actually enjoy a well-thought-out forty-minute sermon from a pastor you trust. You'll find yourself doing more than just accepting the truth of Jesus Christ; you'll also own that truth and defend that truth. You'll find yourself continually opening that toolbox and the arsenal described in the previous chapter.

# WE'RE
# NOT
# HOME
# YET

> He has planted eternity in the human heart, but
> even so, people cannot see the whole scope
> of God's work from beginning to end.

*ECCLESIASTES 3:11 NLT*

**IF YOU EVER RUN INTO SOMEONE** who says he has all the answers, be skeptical. Those who truly know and follow Christ know that's not how it works. Instead, as confident, fully surrendered believers, we acknowledge there are things we don't understand. How could we? God is God, and we're not. So we simply accept the fact that we cannot possibly understand the complete motivations and mechanisms of how the world works.

As a result, we may not fully understand a theological technicality. We may question how a verse in Scripture seems like it contradicts another verse. We may debate and disagree about a biblical timeline, the interpretation of a word, or the inclinations of an apostle. But that's okay. It has to be. Because when we cross the threshold into eternity surrounded by God's glory, everything will all make perfect sense:

> *Now we see things imperfectly, like puzzling reflections in a mirror, but then we will see everything with perfect clarity. All that I know now is partial and incomplete, but then I will know everything completely, just as God now knows me completely (I Corinthians 13:12 NLT).*

Does this short confession sound like a cop-out? As if I just confirmed Christians are following a made-up religion without really digging deep and insisting on having all the facts? Well, that's not the case at all.

Stating it as plainly as possible, God chooses to touch the hearts and minds of individuals at exactly the right time for each person. You may be surprised to hear that when the time is right, you won't insist upon having the complete answer to every question. Oh, you'll still approach life with logic and sound reasoning. You'll continue to develop a practical and prosperous vision for your future. However, instead of looking outward, you'll finally take a chance and look upward, realizing there's more to life than the here and now. You'll finally see that taking the Jesus dare is not intimidating, but rather it's accepting the open hand of a loving Brother. And you'll say, "Oh, I get it. God is calling me."

After all, we are mere humans. Which means we are going to have to admit there are many realities outside our earthly awareness we cannot possibly fully comprehend, including who God is, the moment of creation, the concept of eternity, the location of heaven and hell, and so on.

Eventually each of us needs to come to God as we are: imperfect and eager to be made new.

# COME
# AS YOU
# ARE

> *God demonstrates His own love
> for us in this: While we were still sinners,
> Christ died for us.*

ROMANS 5:8 NIV

**SHOULD A CHURCH HAVE A DRESS CODE?** When my kids were younger, I had a family rule that they couldn't wear anything to church that had words on it. I didn't want something my child was wearing—a logo or clever slogan—to distract from the pastor's sermon or a lesson that God might be trying to teach someone sitting in the next pew.

Looking back, I see that idea was a little shortsighted. While we probably shouldn't wear an Incredible Hulk costume or set our hair on fire in the church sanctuary, God really doesn't care too much about how we look. He's much more concerned about the condition of our hearts and minds. A little respect and reverence are certainly in order, but that's secondary to just showing up and being teachable and reachable.

Frankly, looking around most churches, I think we could use a few more ripped jeans, spiked hairstyles, face tattoos, and piercings. I'm not going to encourage my kids in that area, but the gospel is for everyone. The Bible teaches, "The body is not made up of one part but of many" (I Corinthians 12:14 NIV). When everyone in a congregation looks like they're related to each other, there's probably something missing.

Here's the point: God invites *anyone* at *any time* in *any* condition to come into His presence. That could be *anyplace*, including an office cubicle, schoolyard, back alley, jail cell, mountaintop, desert oasis, or even a church building. You don't have to get cleaned up or gussied up. You don't have to put on a tie, take off your shoes, drink any Kool-Aid, or jump through any hoops. And you certainly don't have to be perfect. Please, please, please. Come as you are.

There's a rumor going around that some people are more worthy than others. And that's just not true. The truth is that *nobody* is worthy. Compared to God, none of us deserve any claims in this life or the next. If you stop and think about it for even a moment, that should be quite clear. We all mess up.

We all suffer from the same affliction. Being broken is part of the human condition.

When we realize our personal shortcomings—our sinful condition—we can feel some relief because that's the first step in addressing the problem. To fix a leak, one has to find the leak. To clean a river, one needs to identify the source of the sewage. Before asking Jesus to cleanse our sins, we have to first confess our sins.

Consider the story of a fisherman named Peter. Early in His ministry, Jesus strolled to the shoreline of the Sea of Galilee where a crowd gathered to hear Him speak. At the water's edge, He saw two boats left by fishermen after a disappointing day of work. Jesus got into Simon Peter's boat and asked to be taken just off shore so He could better address the crowd. When He finished speaking, Jesus told Simon Peter to go out and let down the nets for one more catch. Reluctantly, the tired fisherman did as he was told. The number of fish that suddenly filled those nets almost sunk *both* boats. Simon Peter was aware of Jesus' reputation for miracle making. But at that moment, the fisherman knew without a doubt that he was not worthy to be in the presence of this Miracle Worker.

*When Simon Peter saw this, he fell at Jesus' knees and said, "Go away from me, Lord; I am a sinful man!" For he and all his companions were astonished at the catch of fish they had taken, and so were James and John, the sons of Zebedee, Simon's partners.*

Then Jesus said to Simon, "Don't be afraid; from now on you will fish for people." So they pulled their boats up on shore, left everything and followed Him (Luke 5:8–11 NIV).

Only when Peter confessed his sinfulness—acknowledged his unworthiness—was he capable of dropping his nets, leaving everything behind, and following Jesus. Even for an impulsive fisherman, that's a startling decision. But it turned out to be a pretty good trade.

So, are you worried about being unworthy to receive God's love? Let me repeat, there is no dress code. There is no quantity of fish you have to catch. There is no specific church building in which you have to kneel, lift your arms, or toss half your paycheck in a bucket.

Jesus dares you to come as you are. Yes, there are ideas to unpack and weigh. If you come as you are, you're very likely carrying some habits or routines that you will soon want to recalibrate. But those shortcomings are not keeping you from *pursuing* Jesus and experiencing His love and forgiveness. So keep reading. Are you with me?

Portions excerpted from Jay Payleitner, *If God Were Your Life Coach* (Franklin, TN: Worthy Publishing, 2017), 100-101

# KNOW
# YOU ARE
# LOVABLE

> *See what great love the Father has lavished on us,
> that we should be called children of God!*

*I JOHN 3:1 NIV*

*THE IDEA THAT YOU HAVE* to "clean up your act" before approaching a relationship with Jesus is closely related to another obstacle to seeking His guidance in your life. And it makes me angry.

Way too many people look in the mirror every morning and don't like what they see.

This self-defeating mindset may be one of the great lies permeating today's cultural climate. Especially with our young people.

I'm not talking about physical beauty, although that may be a contributing factor. I'm talking about that feeling of self-loathing or hollowness that leads otherwise healthy people to an epidemic of depression, hopelessness, and paralyzing fear. A sense that they just don't matter. They have nothing to contribute. Nothing to live for. In a word, they feel unlovable.

This self-degradation can manifest itself in obvious, public ways, sometimes even leading to tragic results. Or it can be a quiet suffering kept mostly hidden from the world. At different seasons of life the feeling can diminish or increase, but it's always there, just below the surface.

Actually, almost everyone endures occasional bouts of self-doubt and insecurity. Some can even use those feelings to trigger a little healthy soul searching and a fresh start. But for many, the burdensome belief is ongoing and leads to feelings of hostility toward themselves and toward others.

What causes this attitude? In some cases, those individuals experienced physical or emotional abuse as a child. Mom didn't hold them. Dad was too busy or treated them brutally. Never a kind word was said. Tragedy, loss, or shattered dreams may have swept into their life during a season when they had no place to turn for comfort or support. Addiction, disease, over-medication, and a variety of other factors can feed into this self-destructive mindset.

Statistically, you know people who are barely surviving because they feel unworthy of love. Maybe you've gone through such a season.

Well, good news. Actually, amazing news. You are loved. By the Creator of the universe. Even better, He loves you without any condition. Even if you reject Him, He loves you and wants the very best for you.

God knows you, cares about you, and follows your every move. This idea may be impossible to comprehend, but you are one of God's favorites. And He has big plans for you.

Let that be your new reality. Imagine that you have more to offer than you can even imagine. Special powers He has given you because He loves you so much. The power to love, give, weep, smile, heal, encourage, instruct, comfort, and so much more.

# AND
# YOU'RE
# BEAUTIFUL

> *He has made everything beautiful in its time.*

ECCLESIASTES 3:11 NIV

*LET'S TAKE ANOTHER SWING AT THE IDEA* that too many people look in the mirror and don't like what they see.

May I suggest that even if you don't, God sees you as beautiful?

Now it's very possible that the world—specifically today's beauty-obsessed culture—may *not* see you as beautiful. Fashion magazine editors are not scheduling you for photo shoots. You were not nominated for prom king or queen. Bouncers are not moving the velvet rope allowing you entrance to that exclusive Manhattan dance club.

As a matter of fact, all those commercials for cosmetic surgery, weight-loss products, anti-aging creams, acne medicine, and a wide array of similar products seem to be targeted at you. What's that about?

Well, it's the world saying you're ugly.

Actually, it's other people hoping you'll think that. Thoughtless, coldhearted people. Manipulative people who might profit financially from your thinking that. Or people who might feel better about *themselves* if you think of *yourself* in those terms. People you can't help listening to but probably shouldn't be. It's a cruddy feeling, isn't it?

Here are three quick and compelling realizations that can help eradicate that feeling:

- One, you were made in God's image. That's a core truth found in the very first chapter of the Bible. Genesis 1:27 confirms, "God created mankind in His own image, in the image of God He created them; male and female He created them" (NIV). So whether you're a male or female, you can actually look in the mirror and get a glimpse of the Creator.

- Two, for those who have been redeemed, when God looks at you, He sees the righteousness of His Son. The only ugly things about you—your sins— have been washed away by the blood of Christ.

- Three, you will be part of God's family. A son or daughter of a heavenly Father. And you know He sees you as one of His most precious creations.

God's love for you makes you beautiful. And now you have even more reasons to take the Jesus dare.

# NOW
# FOR
# SOME
# BAD
# NEWS

> *They will throw them into the blazing furnace, where there will be weeping and gnashing of teeth.*

MATTHEW 13:42 NIV

**YES, GOD WELCOMES YOU WITH OPEN ARMS.** He loves you unconditionally. He made you. He cares about you. You are unquestionably beautiful. But before you go skipping down the no-worries trail, let's make sure you don't wander too far from this sober reality check.

When it comes to choosing whether or not to take the Jesus dare, you will want to at least consider the idea that hell is a real place with real suffering. Because if it is, you don't want to go there.

> *The cowardly, the unbelieving, the vile, the murderers, the sexually immoral, those who practice magic arts, the idolaters and all liars—they will be consigned to the fiery lake of burning sulfur. This is the second death (Revelation 21:8 NIV).*

A fiery lake of burning sulfur? Yikes. While some Christians believe that's a literal description of hell, others see it as a literary metaphor. Overall, I'm not sure it matters. (Also, don't expect Satan to show up wearing red or carrying a pitchfork. He's much more devious than that.)

Likewise, heaven may or may not have gold roads and a crystal river as described in Revelation 21 and 22. Not surprisingly, our wildest imagination can't fathom the awesomeness of what's waiting for those who have accepted Christ as their Savior. In the New Testament, we get an unequivocal confirmation that heaven is beyond human understanding:

> *No eye has seen, no ear has heard, and no mind has imagined what God has prepared for those who love Him (I Corinthians 2:9 NLT).*

Some theologians differentiate heaven and hell this way. God is in heaven. He is not in hell.

In other words, if God really exists, you definitely are going to want to hang out with Him in paradise for all eternity. That's something you don't want to miss. After all, eternity is a long time.

The other option is actually worse than a fiery lake of burning sulfur. It's eternal separation from God and His glory.

> *They will be punished with eternal destruction, forever separated from the Lord and from His glorious power (II Thessalonians 1:9 NLT).*

An eternity disconnected from God may not seem like a big, painful ordeal. But mull that idea over for a while, and He might reveal to you how agonizing that would be.

# FOR
## THOSE MORE
## INTERESTED
## IN THE HERE
## AND NOW

*II CORINTHIANS 6:2 NIV*

*IT WOULD BE GREAT IF YOU* intentionally and decisively reserved your spot in heaven today.

But maybe you are so focused on what's going on in this world that the afterlife isn't on your radar screen. You're assuming you've got several decades left and there's no real urgency.

Besides, the previous chapter revealed that heaven is impossible to imagine. When you do try to envision yourself in heaven, all you see is the unappealing idea of sitting on a cloud day after day playing a harp.

Furthermore, most people don't want to think about dying.

Which leaves you pondering the reasonable question, *How does the Jesus dare apply to my life on this planet?*

Well, first, please don't dismiss the importance of your eternal destination. This life is a finger snap compared to all of eternity. Heaven is real. And I recommend confirmed reservations.

But back to the question. It's a good one. So let's take two short chapters to consider the real-world here-and-now advantages of taking the Jesus dare sooner rather than later.

One has to do with eliminating bad stuff. The other is about accentuating good stuff.

# THE
# FREEDOM OF
# SURRENDER

> Jesus replied,
> "Very truly I tell you,
> everyone who sins
> is a slave to sin."

*JOHN 8:34 NIV*

**SORRY, BUT WE'RE GOING TO TALK** a little more about sin. I know, I know. It's not a fun topic.

Just to reconfirm. Sin separates us from God. The tragic result is you are blocked from the eternity in heaven we've been promising. But almost as tragic is this: Your sinful condition prevents you from living your best life and reaching your potential here on earth.

If you're feeling trapped, stuck in a cycle of bad decisions, or frustrated because you're not living up to your expectations, you can trace much of that personal bondage back to sin.

Examples of sin that leads to enslavement are easy to come up with:

- Someone with a habit of lying will spend much of their time and energy lying to cover up the original lies. And worrying about getting caught.

- Sex outside of marriage will open the door to all kinds of diseases, unwanted pregnancies, and suspicions, worries, and intimacy issues with your spouse or future spouse.

- The selfish act of poking at a smartphone screen or video gaming for hours and hours while ignoring the people around you will isolate you from opportunities to love and be loved.

- Being envious of your neighbor's stuff will lead to a life of chasing things and inevitably leaves you with a stack of credit card debt and an empty heart.

- If you dishonor your parents, holiday gatherings that should be filled with joy will instead foster bitterness and ill will. Or loneliness and heartache.

Sin robs the joy from life. Admittedly, you can find sinful stuff that may bring some kind of buzz or ecstasy in the moment, but eventually it all catches up with you. The recklessness of the cheap thrill is not a cliché.

The lure of today's culture only adds to the bondage. Much of what the world recommends takes us further from God's best plan for our lives. Even for the strongest of us, that pressure is inescapable.

All of us have sinned and will sin again. Repercussions are inevitable. If you think you've escaped the fallout of your sins, you are mistaken. While most sins have immediate consequences, some repercussions may not surface for years.

But here's the good news. When you surrender your life to Christ, you receive the gift of the Holy Spirit. And this third member of the Trinity is going to provide an advance warning system to help steer your decision making. Galatians 5:16 puts it this way: "Let the Holy Spirit guide your lives. Then you won't be doing what your sinful nature craves" (NLT).

The result? When you surrender to Christ, you will be more likely to *recognize* sin ahead of time, which in turn should lead you to sin *less frequently* and also sin *less severely*.

Your angry outbursts will be less frequent and less intense. Your tendency to judge will fade, gossip will be less appealing, and you will have more empathy. Lust will lessen. Your self-respect will increase. Also, you may experience a change in the places you go and the people you hang out with. It's all part of the new capacity you will have to discern good and evil. Really.

Altruistic feelings you never expected will surface. Patience with teenagers. Composure at the post office. Generosity to panhandlers who look healthy enough to get a job. When that coworker gets your promotion, rather than suffering envy that eats at your gut, you may even experience a tinge of goodwill.

While these new gifts—superpowers if you will—are immediately available, they may take weeks, months, or even a lifetime to master. Because you live in this world, sin will still be part of your daily life, but it won't have the death grip it once had. Taking the Jesus dare is going to loosen the shackles of sin, giving you a new freedom in Christ, a peace you've never felt before, and a taste of heaven on earth.

Portions excerpted from Jay Payleitner, *If God Were Your Life Coach* (Franklin, TN: Worthy Publishing, 2017), 103-104.

# TRADING YOUR PLAN FOR GOD'S PLAN

> *The mind governed by the flesh
> is death, but the mind governed
> by the Spirit is life and peace.*

ROMANS 8:6 NIV

**SO, ONE EARTHLY BENEFIT OF TAKING** the Jesus dare is that you will be downsizing the seductive and destructive power of sin in your life.

The flip side is even better. You will also be replacing your pretty good plan with God's amazingly awesome plan for your time here on this planet. Accepting Christ as Lord and Savior opens your life to re-imagined meaning and purpose. That includes your motivations, relationships, health, and priorities.

Every aspect of your life will turn a corner:

• Personal beliefs and attitudes guided by the culture—hate, greed, racism, and wickedness—are exchanged for attributes drawn from the character of God: love, generosity, fellowship, and righteousness.

- Instead of panicking about your financial security, you'll trust God to provide. And He will! Everything is His anyway, and He promises to supply your daily bread.

- Instead of expecting your job to be your source of personal fulfillment, you'll find yourself working to give glory to God. Suddenly you'll realize that He has given you gifts and abilities for a purpose beyond yourself. The entire focus of your work and career changes.

- If you're married, your plan was to count on that relationship for companionship and romance. If you are a follower of Christ, that's still the plan. Research reveals that married couples who attend church together have better and more frequent sex. Even more significantly, you would see marriage as a gift reflecting the sacrificial love found in the relationship of Christ and His church. Ephesians 5:25 describes that correlation: "Husbands, love your wives, just as Christ loved the church and gave Himself up for her" (NIV).

- In your plan, family is about providing security, care, and love for one another. But in God's plan, families are the building blocks of communities, nations, and the world. That was clearly established in one of the first directives God gave to Adam and Eve in the Garden of Eden. In Genesis 1:28 we read, "God blessed them and said to them, 'Be fruitful and increase in number; fill the earth and subdue it'" (NIV).

- In God's plan, friends and acquaintances don't just expand your worldview and provide alternate perspectives. Relationships build the kingdom of God here on earth, providing a taste of heaven.

- Health and physical fitness don't just allow you to play hard and live long. They give you strength to work for God, offering your body as a "living sacrifice" (Romans 12:1 NIV).

- Education doesn't just lead to knowledge, respect, and influence. It equips you to point others to God.

- From your human perspective, tragedies and failures lead to sorrow, regret, and shame. At best, we hope the setbacks of life might serve as lessons or teach perseverance. But in God's plan, even the worst misfortunes will ultimately be used for good. It may be hard to imagine, but He promises to turn every affliction and heartbreak into blessings. It may take time, but you can trust that God is in control. Eventually, God will reveal a bigger picture allowing you to see how He always brings light to the darkness.

Personal character. Financial security. Career. Family. Friends. Health. Education. Even tragedies. In every facet of life, the best the world can offer is chicken feed compared to what God has in store for those who call on His name.

In God's plan, instead of living for yourself, you live for Him, even going so far as to put others ahead of yourself.

Don't worry, you come out way ahead.

# WORTH
# MENTIONING

> *Oh, how great are God's riches and wisdom and knowledge! How impossible it is for us to understand His decisions and His ways!*

ROMANS 11:33 NLT

**OH YEAH, AFTER TAKING THE JESUS DARE,** you just may find one or two bonus surprises waiting right around the corner.

Those added benefits are not guaranteed. You also may not believe such things even exist until you experience them for yourself—and it might take several occurrences to convince you. I also hesitate to bring it up because you may shake your ahead and think, *That's ridiculous.* But here goes.

Your eyes will be opened to an invisible world. Specifically, to miracles and angels.

As a new creation, you'll start to realize that some of the nice, serendipitous, and previously unexplainable occurrences in our world are not mere coincidences. They are a direct result of God's intervention. Healings.

Mysterious voices. Tragedies averted. Heroic strangers who disappear when the paramedics arrive. Financial windfalls for the exact amount needed for an emergency. Visits to heaven. Broken marriages restored. Lost children led to safety. Loved ones reunited.

Sure, some remarkable events can be explained. But some can't. The mugger who said he was scared away by "two giant dudes who showed up out of nowhere." The little girl who was "pulled out of traffic by a mysterious force." The surgeon who "can't explain what happened to the tumor." The child who precisely describes a place he has never been or a person he has never met.

Again, it's okay to be skeptical. But also don't be totally surprised. Whether you believe it or not, miracles occur every day. Not just people doing nice things or some athlete making a "miraculous" play. But God supernaturally contradicting the laws of nature to express His love or open our eyes to His power.

Also, angels are mentioned more than two hundred times in the Bible. For example, Psalm 91:11–12 says, "He will order His angels to protect you wherever you go. They will hold you up with their hands" (NLT).

Hebrews 1:14 says, "Are not all angels ministering spirits sent to serve those who will inherit salvation?" (NIV). And my favorite, Hebrews 13:2 (NLT) reminds us, "Don't forget to show hospitality to strangers, for some who have done this have entertained angels without realizing it!"

Once again, God's great plan is way beyond our comprehension. But still His mysterious ways often provide moments of unexpected protection, guidance, and comfort to us mere mortals. Especially those who call Him "Father."

# THE
# PROBLEM
# WITH
# RELIGION

> *Woe to you, scribes and Pharisees, hypocrites! For you are like whitewashed tombs, which outwardly appear beautiful, but within are full of dead people's bones and all uncleanness.*

MATTHEW 23:27 ESV

*IF THE RELUCTANCE* to "join a religion" has you hesitant to take the Jesus dare, I understand. You are not alone.

The atrocities committed in the name of the world's religions would fill a history book. In fact, they do. I'm especially sad to confirm that many crimes and evil deeds have been committed by individuals or groups who called themselves Christians. The list includes the Crusades, the Salem witch trials, and slavery in America.

But before making any sweeping judgments, you'll want to dig a bit deeper. Further study reveals many cruelties attributed to Christians were committed by those who *claimed* to be religious but acted with evil intent. What's more, their wickedness was ultimately thwarted by authentic followers of Christ.

For example, millions were killed during the Crusades, which arguably lasted for almost half a millennium, from the eleventh to the sixteenth centuries. The "holy" war sanctioned by the Latin church finally came to an end when the money-making schemes of church leadership were exposed, the printing press allowed God's Word to be widely read, and the Reformation took hold among the biblically literate.

In 1692, Salem village's controversial minister, Samuel Parris—who never finished his degree in theology—was the primary accuser for the nineteen "witches" tried without counsel and hanged on Gallows Hill. But many local Christian leaders are credited with ending the dubious accusations and subsequently protecting the rights of the accused.

The two and a half centuries of slavery in America (1619–1865) began when 12.5 million Africans were shipped to the New World. Of that number, 10.7 million survived the voyage, marking the first of several generations living in the bondage of slavery. Leading up to the Civil War, Jefferson Davis, president of the Confederacy, as well as Generals Robert E. Lee and Stonewall Jackson were among many who worshipped as Christians yet justified slavery, even citing biblical history. But it was articulate and passionate Christians like Harriet Beecher Stowe, Harriet Tubman, William Wilberforce, Charles Spurgeon, Sojourner Truth, and Frederick Douglass who trailblazed the abolitionist movement.

The above three examples of historical atrocities suggest that the problem is not with religion. The problem is with the nature of humanity. Sometimes we choose good. Sometimes we choose evil.

Which brings up an even more significant point. *The presence of good and evil may very well prove the existence of God.* How's that? Well, as soon as we identify an act as good or evil, we've made a moral judgment. And no human has the ability to determine what is good or evil. That would be unfair to the rest of the 7 billion inhabitants of earth. The only fair way to define *good* is to establish a standard outside of the human world. In other words, God.

Said another way, a universal morality can only be based on the character of God. As we stated in an earlier chapter, God is love, truth, mercy, respect, justice, and peace. That's the only standard that works. Morality—distinguishing between that which is evil and that which is good—requires a perfect prototype. Then, when you hold an action or thought up against that perfect standard, it either measures up…or it doesn't.

It follows, then, that religion pointing to God with clarity and integrity has value. But at any time and place, religious practices can be tainted by the world. The Bible confirms there can very well be a problem with religion:

> *"If anyone thinks he is religious and does not bridle his tongue but deceives his heart, this person's religion is worthless. Religion that is pure and undefiled before God the Father is this: to visit orphans and widows in their affliction, and to keep oneself unstained from the world" (James 1:26–27 ESV).*

All that to say, the practice of religion requires checks and balances—accountability to stay protected from the distractions and temptations of the world. It's too easy for individuals, congregations, and entire denominations to be caught up in looking good, knowing the right words, feeling holy, and even doing very good deeds. Sometimes fooling others; often fooling themselves.

Still, there are clear benefits to authentic believers rallying for a common cause. It's true that one person can make a difference, but it's people working *together* that really gets things done.

That's why religion is organized. Maybe too organized for some. But that doesn't make it evil. Even the original rallying cry of the early church called members to hold each other accountable and aspire to honor, generosity, and integrity. Peter taught and pleaded with the people to "save yourselves from this corrupt generation" (Acts 2:40 NIV). Thousands were baptized and devoted themselves to fellowship, prayer, and sharing their worldly possessions.

It may help to think of religion not as a set of rules or beliefs but as a process. Learning. Growing. Welcoming. Encouraging. Admitting our human frailty. Broken people helping other broken people see the big picture. That process of mutual accountability leads to asking important questions about God's purpose for our lives, the responsibilities that come with being heavenly minded, and how members can make a difference here on earth.

So, because history should not be ignored, let's remain vigilant regarding those church bodies and individuals in church leadership who dishonor God with their thoughts and actions. Never forget it was religious zealots who arranged for Jesus' trial, lashing, and death on a cross.

But also never forget that religion—specifically the Christian faith—also gave the world the YMCA, the Salvation Army, Prison Fellowship, St. Jude's Hospital, The Mayo Clinic, Johns Hopkins Hospital, Habitat for Humanity, World Relief, Compassion International, Leprosy Missions, Food for the Poor, Open Doors USA, Alcoholics Anonymous, Amnesty International, Harvard, Yale, Princeton, Cambridge, Oxford, the Magna Carta, the Declaration of Independence, Handel, Bach, Mozart, Beethoven, Stravinsky, Schubert, Michelangelo, Raphael, Rembrandt, da Vinci, Galileo, Johannes Kepler, Isaac Newton,

Marconi, George Washington Carver, Jane Addams, Clara Barton, Lech Walesa, Louis Braille, Dr. Martin Luther King Jr., and tens of thousands of doctors and medical professionals who travel to minister to the poorest of the poor every year on medical mission trips.

Is there a problem with religion? The problem might be that too many people these days, intentionally or otherwise, are giving it a bad rap.

# SIDE
# WITH THE
# SMART
# PEOPLE

> The fear of the LORD is the beginning of wisdom; all who follow His precepts have good understanding. To Him belongs eternal praise.

PSALM 111:10 NIV

**THE SMARTEST PEOPLE ALIVE TODAY** seem to be talk show hosts. Everything they say gets applause. (Or maybe it's the flashing sign in the studio that instructs the audience.)

Or perhaps the smartest people alive are tech geniuses. Because they use their smarts to become gazillionaires.

Or maybe college professors. Because they use their smarts to tell *other* people how to be smart.

Or maybe politicians. Because they use their smarts to decide how to spend your money on their own projects.

Well, up until about a century ago, the smartest people on the planet spent much of their time reflecting on the character of God. These deep thinkers were well respected and quoted often. They didn't do it for the money. They weren't motivated by fame. They were simply seeking and sharing truth.

Following are a few quotes from several recognized geniuses of history. We can't know the depth of their personal relationship with God, but we do know they were seeking answers. Maybe their deep thoughts will lead to your own deep thoughts about God as our loving Father who sent His Son to earth on our behalf.

*A little knowledge leads a man away from God, but a great deal brings him back.*
FRANCIS BACON

*If God were small enough to be understood, He would not be big enough to be worshipped.*
EVELYN UNDERHILL

*Jesus does not give recipes that show the way to God
as other teachers of religion do, He is Himself the way.*
KARL BARTH

*He who has God finds he lacks
nothing; God alone suffices.*
TERESA OF AVILA

*Believe that God loves you as you cannot conceive;
that He loves you with your sin, in your sin.*
FYODOR DOSTOYEVSKY

*The longer I live, the more convincing proofs
I see of this truth—that God governs in the
affairs of men. And if a sparrow cannot fall to
the ground without His notice, is it probable
that an empire can rise without His aid?*
BENJAMIN FRANKLIN

*Dare to love God without mediator or veil.*
RALPH WALDO EMERSON

*I want to know how God created this world. I
am not interested in this or that phenomenon,
in the spectrum of this or that element. I want
to know His thoughts; the rest are details.*
ALBERT EINSTEIN

*One, on God's side, is a majority.*
WENDELL PHILLIPS

*The Almighty has His own purposes.*
ABRAHAM LINCOLN

*And now here is my secret, a very simple secret:*
*It is only with the heart that one can see rightly;*
*what is essential is invisible to the eye.*
ANTOINE DE SAINT-EXUPÉRY

*Let us weigh the gain and the loss in wagering that*
*God is. Let us estimate these two chances. If you*
*gain, you gain all; if you lose, you lose nothing.*
*Wager, then, without hesitation that He is.*
BLAISE PASCAL

*God moves in a mysterious way, His wonders to perform.*
WILLIAM COWPER

---

*Man considers the actions, but God weighs the intentions.*
THOMAS À KEMPIS

---

*Lift your heart and let it rest upon Jesus and you
are instantly in a sanctuary though it be a Pullman
berth or a factory or a kitchen. You can see God from
anywhere if your mind is set to love and obey Him.*
A.W. TOZER

*God grant me the serenity to accept the things I*
*cannot change, the courage to change the things*
*I can, and the wisdom to know the difference.*
REINHOLD NIEBUHR

*I feel something within that lives to God, that*
*delights in God, that cannot exist without*
*God, that must be derived from God.*
JANET COLQUHOUN

*Love is the foolishness of men, and the wisdom of God.*
VICTOR HUGO

*God united human nature and the divine nature in
the Person of the Word, the greatest work of all.*
THOMAS AQUINAS

*Many pass for saints on earth whose souls are in hell.*
MARTIN LUTHER

*A comprehended god is no god.*
JOHN CHRYSOSTOM

*The nature of God is a circle of which the center is*
*everywhere and the circumference is nowhere.*
*EMPEDOCLES*

*The Christian ideal has not been tried and found wanting.*
*It has been found difficult; and left untried.*
*G. K. CHESTERTON*

*Nothing else is needed to quiet all your fears*
*but just this: that God is. Nothing can separate*
*you from His love, absolutely nothing.*
*HANNAH WHITALL SMITH*

*When we find out an idea by whose intervention
we discover the connexion of two others,
this is a revelation from God to us by the
voice of reason: for we then come to know
a truth that we did not know before.*

JOHN LOCKE

*When Christ died, He died for you individually just as
much as if you had been the only man in the world.*

C. S. LEWIS

*God comes to thee, not as in the dawning of
the day, not as in the bud of the spring, but as
the sun at noon, to illustrate all shadows.*

JOHN DONNE

*I've read the last page of the Bible. It's*
*all going to turn out all right.*
BILLY GRAHAM


*What a mercy it is that it is not your hold of Christ*
*that saves you, but His hold of you!*
CHARLES SPURGEON


*God exists whether or not men may choose to*
*believe in Him. The reason why many people do not*
*believe in God is not so much that it is intellectually*
*impossible to believe in God, but because belief*
*in God forces that thoughtful person to face the*
*fact that he is accountable to such a God.*
ROBERT A. LAIDLAW

*God gave us the gift of life; it is up to us to*
*give ourselves the gift of living well.*
*VOLTAIRE*

---

*Trust completely in God, and when He brings*
*you to a new opportunity of adventure,*
*offering it to you, see that you take it.*
*OSWALD CHAMBERS*

Sure, you can find philosophers who don't believe in God. Friedrich Nietzsche and Karl Marx come to mind.

But the point of this chapter is to encourage you not to be intimidated by a handful of narcissistic secular atheists who imply that anyone who follows Christ must have checked their brain at the door. The greatest thinkers of history would suggest that is simply not true.

# INTELLECTUAL
# ARGUMENTS

> *You will know the truth,*
> *and the truth will set you free.*

JOHN 8:32 NIV

*FOR SOME READERS, THIS CHAPTER* may be pivotal. Maybe you're one of those inquisitive folk who needs a solid dose of logic, scientific data, and historic proof before avowing Jesus is who He says He is.

Your heart is yearning to say yes to Jesus. To be part of God's family. To be free from the bondage of sin. To know an eternal purpose and have confidence in your eternal destination. But you need that hard evidence.

I get it. Intellectual validation was also one of the pieces to the puzzle I needed before I could, as an adult, give my life to Christ.

I'm pleased to report an abundance of evidence exists. Evidence that falls under the category of irrefutable, consistent, and compelling. Scholars, archaeologists, and historians have presented volumes of research and discoveries supporting the reliability of the Scriptures. That includes well-documented books like *The Case for Christ* by Lee Strobel, *Evidence That Demands a Verdict* by Josh McDowell, *Unshakable Foundations* by Norman Geisler and Peter Bocchino, and *The Incomparable Christ* by J. Oswald Sanders.

When it came to my own faith journey, I had to gather just enough verification to satisfy my own curiosity and override my remaining skepticism. You might need more. If that's the case, please grab some or all of the resources listed above. It's really okay if you need to dig deeper before taking the Jesus dare. But please don't prolong your investigation.

In any case, keep this list of books handy. After taking the dare you may discover a surprising hunger to find out more about your new Savior and King.

With all that in mind, here's what we're going to do the rest of this chapter. I am going to share the four revelations that enabled me to intellectually accept Jesus' true identity and recognize my need to surrender to Him. See if they resonate with your inquiring mind.

## MESSIANIC PROPHECIES

History shows that the Old Testament was written long before Jesus was born. But there are literally hundreds of prophecies in the Old Testament that point very specifically to where, when, and how Jesus would be born, live, die, and rise from the dead. For instance, seven hundred years before Christ, Micah 5:2 predicted the Messiah would come from a tiny town called Bethlehem. The book written by the prophet Isaiah predicted the virgin birth, Jesus' miracles, and the exact circumstances of His crucifixion and burial. And so on.

## RECENT ARCHAEOLOGICAL DISCOVERIES

Every few years, like clockwork, secular scientists are stunned to uncover new evidence supporting the biblical record. Meanwhile, Christians stand by saying, "We knew it all along." For example, critics had been saying for centuries that Old Testament cities such as Petra, Ubar, and Ebla were merely myths. But modern technology and determined archaeologists have found them buried in the desert sand. In 1947, a Bedouin goatherder came upon a cave containing jars filled with ancient manuscripts. Those Dead Sea Scrolls confirmed the accuracy of much of today's Old Testament.

## THE PRACTICAL APPLICATION OF THE TEN COMMANDMENTS

At first glance, the Ten Commandments may seem a little random. Half of them explicitly forbid destructive human failings, activities such as stealing, lying, murder, envy, and adultery. Two commandments appear to be based on the sentimental ideas of honoring your parents and taking Sundays off. Unmistakably, the first three commandments get very specific about the character of God: He is the one and only. He needs to be a priority in our lives. Even His name is powerful.

Despite what some naysayers may suggest, the stone tablets Moses brought down from Mt. Sinai are much more than an antiquated list of do's and don't. Their application is surprisingly far-reaching.

First, they give us something to shoot for, clear descriptors of right and wrong. Second, as benchmarks for human behavior, they confirm that we all fall short of God's standards. Third, collectively they render a comprehensive formula for life. I submit that every relevant law or rule ever conceived just might be covered in the Ten Commandments. That includes criminal law, property law, classroom conduct, playground policies, family rules, and every clause of the U. S. Constitution. At the core of any reputable law you'll find ideals like honesty, sharing, valuing life, respecting property, and honoring relationships with family, neighbors, and God.

Is that an overstatement? I would challenge you to turn to Exodus 20:1–17 and meditate on the "Decalogue." You'll discover a profound and universal list no mere human could have written.

## THE MARTYRDOM OF THE APOSTLES

How do we know Jesus was resurrected? I've read many proofs, but let me share just one. The twelve apostles (and many others) claim to have seen Jesus alive after the crucifixion. Could they have been lying? Yes, I suppose. Except that eleven of them died brutal deaths as martyrs because they insisted that Jesus rose from the dead and hung out with them for forty days after that first Easter. Why would these men die for a lie? They wouldn't! If Jesus died on the cross and stayed buried in the tomb, those men would have scattered, and the entire Christian faith would have ended then and there. Instead, their ongoing commitment to this new faith movement has become one of the great proofs that Jesus rose from the dead and still lives today.

Do you still have questions? I hope so. The Jesus dare should not be taken lightly. Beyond digging into additional scholarly research, I hope you kick around these ideas with family and friends. The claims of Christ can stand up to any sincere and honorable debate.

Hey, we're into the home stretch. Just a few pages left. Thanks for your diligence and perseverance.

Portions excerpted from Jay Payleitner, *10 Conversations Kids Need to Have with Their Dad* (Eugene, OR: Harvest House, 2014), 174-175.

# IT'S A TRUSTWORTHY PLAN

**ONE OF THE GREAT STUMBLING BLOCKS** for intelligent folks—like you—is that you can't imagine anyone or anything having the ability to conceive and orchestrate this vast universe in which we live. And, in many ways, it does seem impossible. The idea of a Creator God in control of everything that exists is beyond our comprehension.

But what's the alternative? Could our entire existence be a random accident? That may be even harder to imagine. The entire universe can't possibly be an arbitrary and accidental hodgepodge, can it? Admittedly, our human minds have limits, but intuitively we recognize an order to the world around us. The North Star points north. Apples fall from trees to make more trees. The hungry lion chases down the weakest gazelle. Humans and animals take in oxygen and exhale carbon dioxide, while trees and other plants do just the opposite. The 23.4% tilt of the earth's axis creates the four seasons. Rainbows follow the storm.

The more we know, the more science confirms that the universe is not a heap of disjointed debris. Building blocks exist at all levels of creation. Amino acids. DNA. Cells. Planets. Galaxies. There is organization. The world is not free-falling into oblivion without rhyme or reason.

At first glance, some lives and some cultures may seem to be in chaos, but a closer examination reveals hierarchies and human motivations, for good or evil. A tsunami or a volcano may appear arbitrary to those impacted by the tragedy, but geologists can readily explain and often predict the seismic activity deep below the earth's surface that precipitates such events. It might not seem fair when bad things happen to good people, but over time illnesses and calamities befall every family and culture. The Bible teaches, "[God] gives His sunlight to both the evil and the good, and He sends rain on the just and the unjust alike" (Matthew 5:45 NLT).

What's more, much human suffering is not arbitrary at all. Sometimes innocent people suffer as a result of terrible human choices. Examples include people killed by drunk drivers, school shootings, and genocide ordered by tyrannical dictators. Sometimes human suffering is a result of a choice made by people who willingly took the risk. That includes climbers who freeze to death on the slopes of Mt. Everest, boxers with subdural hematomas, or individuals infected with sexually transmitted diseases.

In God's vast eternal plan, however, joy far outweighs sorrow. That covenant of joy extends far beyond anything you can imagine. You may think your greatest joys bubble up from your experience with nature, family, love, art, and other visceral experiences. That's a reasonable conclusion. But please note that all those joy-givers flow directly or indirectly from God. Plus, earthly joy is a mere hint of what can be in store for your future. In other words, you ain't seen nuthin' yet.

Joy and sorrow in this world are temporary. But God's agenda delivers permanent, unending joy. As Jesus Himself said, "You have sorrow now, but I will see you again, and your hearts will rejoice, and no one will take your joy from you" (John 16:22 ESV).

Even though our human mind can't fit all the pieces together, the puzzle still merges into a meaningful, organized image. God sees it all. In fact, He is the Designer and Caretaker.

In the midst of that great scheme…is you. And you matter. That's right. The Creator of the universe—who spins our galaxy and designs an infinite variety of snowflakes—cares about you. He knows everything about you, even the exact number of hairs on your head (Luke 12:7). He knows your thoughts, hopes, and dreams. He wants you to "cast all your anxiety on Him" (I Peter 5:7 NIV).

Wonderfully, you can trust God with every decision. Including what to have for breakfast tomorrow and all the more difficult decisions you may have later that day or that decade.

So that's the dare for this chapter: decide whom to trust. Would you surrender your entire well-being to the whims of your neighbor, your pastor, or your work-mate? Certainly not. Your parents or beloved family members? Closer, but still no. Can you trust your own self to gather 100 percent complete information and make 100 percent perfect decisions? All you have to do is recall a few incidents in high school (or just last week) to confirm that your mere human instincts and lack of complete knowledge may occasionally lead you down the wrong path.

For your own well-being, Jesus dares you to put your future in the hands of Someone who knows the future. Someone who has your absolute best interest in mind.

# THE
# BIG
# YES

> *Jesus looked at them and said, "With man this is impossible, but with God all things are possible."*

MATTHEW 19:26 NIV

**FOLLOWING UP ON THE LAST CHAPTER,** these next few paragraphs may convey a startling revelation. Here it is: The biggest question you may have to answer is "Do you believe in God?" If an all-powerful, all-knowing, all-present Creator exists, any other question is pretty meaningless.

Atheists love to stir up trouble by asking all kinds of silly questions about the Bible and God's character. You've heard some of them. You may have even asked some of them.

- *Can God create a rock so big that not even He can lift it?*

- *Where did Cain's wife come from?*

- *If God is all-powerful, why doesn't He simply destroy Satan?*

- *Why didn't the lions eat the zebras on Noah's ark?*

- *Why didn't Jonah drown inside the big fish?*

- *Why didn't Jesus come today so that mass communication would spread His message farther and faster?*

These questions, of course, reflect frivolous human efforts to find a supposed flaw. But such questions posed as theological stumpers are actually quite trivial and inconsequential when compared with the bigger question: Does God exist?

If God exists, we can be sure of two things: He can do anything He wants, and we shouldn't expect to understand His motives. Because…well, He's God. He is now, always has been, and always will be in control.

So, if you say yes to God, then you can trust that all your unanswerable questions have answers. Right?

We can trust in God's infinite love and infinite ability. All the impossible stuff in the Bible is actually possible. There's no real reason to debate whether God created the world in six days or six billion years. The virgin birth, Jesus' miracles, and the resurrection no longer have to be explained. God's plan is unfolding perfectly.

He doesn't need our help. But He does want our loyalty and trust. That choice He is leaving up to each one of us.

# FINAL
# BARRIERS

> *If God is for us, who can be against us?*

ROMANS 8:31 NIV

**DID WE COVER EVERYTHING?** Did we cover enough? We've presented our evidence and arguments logically, emotionally, culturally, historically, spiritually, and practically. Some chapters certainly impacted you more than others. If you pass this book on to someone else, don't be surprised if the chapter you thought was only mildly interesting blows that person's mind.

In writing this short book, I wanted to make sure to provide enough evidence to convict the much younger and more cynical twentysomething version of myself. Mission accomplished. You see, I always believed in God. But I didn't really grasp how my sin kept me disconnected from Him—in the present and for eternity. *Wasn't it God's job to forgive me?* That was my stumbling block. Coming to truly understand my need for grace—that Jesus had to pay the ransom for my sins—was the major turning point for me.

On the other hand, I have a friend who needed to analyze sin and salvation from an intellectual and legal standpoint. If that's a hurdle for you, I hope we presented enough data. There's more out there if you need it.

Another friend who had been raised Jewish finally accepted Jesus of Nazareth as the Messiah after seeing how dozens of prophecies in the Tanakh (Old Testament) pointed to the life of Christ.

Coming to accept Christ is troublesome for many because it seems like they would be turning their back on their family or culture. If that's you, you may need to find an extra dose of courage and personal resolve.

Others find faith in Jesus unreasonable because they think, *All this church stuff and all these authoritarian rules are going to ruin my life.* I understand that line of thought, but it couldn't be further from the truth. Well-grounded rules actually make life easier.

Of course, some in today's culture make light of the Bible as a myth or folktale and thereby claim intellectual superiority over those who have "drunk the Kool-Aid." I urge you to dismiss that idea straightaway. Few educated historians doubt the historical authenticity or validity of the Bible.

Some people don't feel like they can ever be good enough to know Jesus personally. They've made too many mistakes. They've sunk too far. They think, *How could God love someone like me?* Because of their poor self-image or their difficult past, they feel like they have to "clean up their act" before opening a Bible, praying, or walking into a church. If that's you, you may want to reread the chapter giving you permission to come as you are.

If you're still standing behind a giant wall, feeling separated from God's love and Jesus' gift of grace, then I apologize. You've invested a few dollars and a few hours, and I didn't deliver as promised. If you feel called but still can't take the *dare* then maybe you need to talk to a real live person, someone who might be able to help you sort out your concerns. You could even track me down through my website: jaypayleitner.com. Actually, I hope to hear from you. It's that important.

# TAKE
# THE
# DARE

**HERE'S THE BEST NEWS** I could possibly deliver: you can take the Jesus dare right now.

You don't have to wait until you have the whole thing figured out. You're only responsible for what you *do* know. We've been trying to be as thorough as possible. But we also are committed to keeping this book short enough to be read in a week or less. Maybe even one night.

Admittedly, some parts of what you've been reading—God's plan straight from the Bible—can be difficult to understand, and that might be a little frustrating. There's a quote attributed to Mark Twain that makes me smile and helps me deal with that idea:

*It ain't those parts of the Bible that I can't understand that bother me, it is the parts that I do understand.*

Frankly, I'm not sure if Mr. Twain ever took the Jesus dare. But his point is well taken. He's confirming that the Bible is not just another book. It's inspired. It's compelling. It's invitational. It contains plans and guidance that need to be observed. If you find yourself put off by the bloody battles, weird rules in Leviticus, confusing names, and the sheer size of the book itself, I urge you to set aside those distractions. Soon enough you'll have the power to see how it all fits together as part of the bigger picture.

If you've read this little book from the beginning, we're not suggesting that you have accumulated every answer to every question ever asked. But you do have all the information you need. And now you have a decision to make. We've been calling it the Jesus dare, but really it's not that daring. If you've been following along and nodding your head, it should be fairly easy.

Do you agree or disagree with the following straight-forward statement? Can you make it a prayer?

*Dear God, it's pretty clear that nobody's perfect. We're all sinners. Because of that, no mere human is worthy of hanging out with You. Death is inevitable.*

*When I die, somebody has to pay for my sin. If that's on me, I don't want to imagine how I would be spending eternity. Thankfully, You love me enough to provide a way out. You sent Your only Son to live perfectly on earth and pay the penalty for my sin on the cross. It cost Him everything. But amazingly, that ticket to heaven cost me nothing. I just have to accept that gift. With that understanding, I trust You as Savior and Lord. Come into my life and guide me so that my life can give You glory. Amen.*

Got it? Done deal? Challenge met? Welcome to the family.

There are two things I would urge you to do very soon. One, tell somebody about this decision you just made. Two, start a journal. Nothing fancy. Just record the changes you see in your life. Looking back a few months or years from now, you will probably be amazed at how God will have worked in you and through you.

Also, if you have time, drop me a note. I love hearing from new brothers and sisters in Christ.

# ENCOURAGING BIBLE VERSES TO STRENGTHEN YOUR FAITH

But he said to me, "My grace is sufficient for you, for my power is made perfect in weakness." Therefore I will boast all the more gladly of my weaknesses, so that the power of Christ may rest upon me. For the sake of Christ, then, I am content with weaknesses, insults, hardships, persecutions, and calamities. For when I am weak, then I am strong.

*II CORINTHIANS 12:9-10 ESV*

For I can do everything through Christ, who gives me strength.

*PHILIPPIANS 4:13 NLT*

Be strong and courageous. Do not fear or be in dread of them, for it is the Lord your God who goes with you. He will not leave you or forsake you.

*DEUTERONOMY 31:6 ESV*

But those who trust in the Lord will find new strength. They will soar high on wings like eagles. They will run and not grow weary. They will walk and not faint.

*ISAIAH 40:31 NLT*

No temptation has overtaken you but such as is common to man; and God is faithful, who will not allow you to be tempted beyond what you are able, but with the temptation will provide the way of escape also, so that you will be able to endure it.

*I CORINTHIANS 10:13 NASB*

The Lord is my strength and my song, and he has become my salvation; this is my God, and I will praise him, my father's God, and I will exalt him.

*EXODUS 15:2 ESV*

Do not fear, for I am with you; Do not anxiously look about you, for I am your God. I will strengthen you, surely I will help you, Surely I will uphold you with My righteous right hand.

*ISAIAH 41:10 NASB*

Be strong in the Lord and in His mighty power.

*EPHESIANS 6:10 NLT*

For the Lord your God is going with you! He will fight for you against your enemies, and He will give you victory!

*DEUTERONOMY 20:4 NLT*

Be strong and courageous! Do not tremble or be dismayed,
for the Lord your God is with you wherever you go.

*JOSHUA 1:9 NASB*

For God gave us a spirit not of fear but
of power and love and self-control.

*II TIMOTHY 1:7 ESV*

Come to Me, all who are weary and
heavy-laden, and I will give you rest.

*MATTHEW 11:28 NASB*

See, God has come to save me. I will trust in Him and not be afraid.
The Lord God is my strength and my song; He has given me victory.

*ISAIAH 12:2 NLT*

He gives power to the faint, and to him who
has no might he increases strength.

*ISAIAH 40:29 ESV*

The Lord is my light and my salvation—so why
should I be afraid? The Lord is my fortress, protecting
me from danger, so why should I tremble?

*PSALM 27:1 NLT*

# ABOUT THE AUTHOR

Prior to becoming a best-selling author and national speaker, *JAY PAYLEITNER* served as a freelance radio producer for a wide range of movements and ministry leaders including Josh McDowell, Chuck Colson, The Salvation Army, Bible League, Voice of the Martyrs, and National Center for Fathering.

As a family advocate, life pundit, and humorist, Jay has sold more than a half-million books including *52 Things Kids Need from a Dad*, *Love Notes from God*, and *What If God Wrote Your Bucket List?*

As a national speaker, Jay engages audiences at mens' events, marriage retreats, fundraisers, writers' conferences, and creative training sessions. He has spoken at Moody Bible Institute's Pastors Conference and Iron Sharpens Iron conferences in ten states. Jay also served as executive director of the Illinois Fatherhood Initiative.

Jay and his high school sweetheart, Rita, live in the Chicago area where they raised five awesome kids, loved on ten foster babies, and are cherishing grandparenthood. There's much more at jaypayleitner.com.

## ALSO FROM JAY PAYLEITNER

52 Things Kids Need from a Dad
Love Notes from God
What If God Wrote Your Bucket List?
What If God Wrote Your To-Do List?
Once Upon a Tandem
52 Things Wives Need from Their Husbands
52 Things Husbands Need from Their Wives
The One Year Life Verse Devotional
365 Ways to Say "I Love You" to Your Kids
One-Minute Devotions for Dads
52 Things Daughters Need from Their Dad
52 Things Sons Need from Their Dad
Do Something Beautiful
Lifeology
If God Gave Your Graduation Speech
If God Wrote Your Birthday Card
If God Were Your Life Coach
The Dad Manifesto
How to Disciple Men
What If God Wrote Your Shopping List?
52 Ways to Connect as a Couple
101 Things Great Dads Do

*Take delight*
*in the* Lord, *and*
*He will give you*
*the desires of*
*your heart.*

—PSALM 37:4 NIV

LIVE YOUR FAITH

*Dear Friend,*

This book was prayerfully crafted with you, the reader, in mind—every word, every sentence, every page— was thoughtfully written, designed, and packaged to encourage you...right where you are this very moment. At DaySpring, our vision is to see every person experience the life-changing message of God's love. So, as we worked through rough drafts, design changes, edits, and details, we prayed for you to deeply experience His unfailing love, indescribable peace, and pure joy. It is our sincere hope that through these Truth-filled pages your heart will be blessed, knowing that God cares about you—your desires and disappointments, your challenges and dreams.

*He knows. He cares. He loves you unconditionally.*

**BLESSINGS!**
**THE DAYSPRING BOOK TEAM**

---